INVISIBLE WORLDS

# Inside Animals

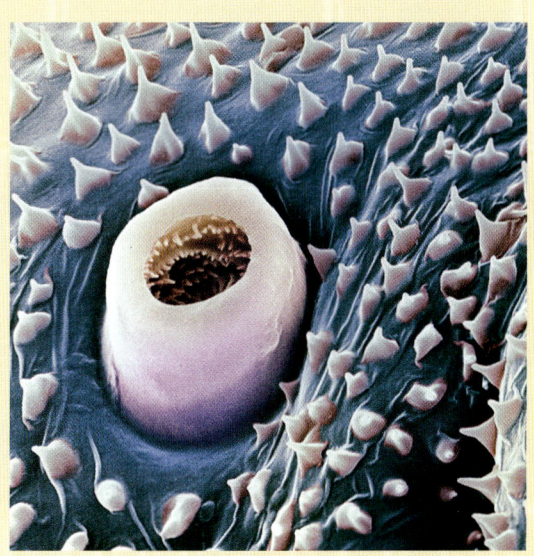

Jen Green

Copyright © 2011 Marshall Cavendish Corporation

Published by Marshall Cavendish Benchmark
An imprint of Marshall Cavendish Corporation

All rights reserved.

No part of this publication may be reproduced, stored in a retrieval system or transmitted, in any form or by any means, electronic, mechanical, photocopying, recording, or otherwise, without the prior permission of the copyright owner. Request for permission should be addressed to the Publisher, Marshall Cavendish Corporation, 99 White Plains Road, Tarrytown, NY 10591. Tel: (914) 332-8888, fax: (914) 332-1888.

Website: www.marshallcavendish.us

This publication represents the opinions and views of the author based on Jen Green's personal experience, knowledge, and research. The information in this book serves as a general guide only. The author and publisher have used their best efforts in preparing this book and disclaim liability rising directly and indirectly from the use and application of this book.

Other Marshall Cavendish Offices:
Marshall Cavendish International (Asia) Private Limited, 1 New Industrial Road, Singapore 536196 • Marshall Cavendish International (Thailand) Co Ltd. 253 Asoke, 12th Flr, Sukhumvit 21 Road, Klongtoey Nua, Wattana, Bangkok 10110, Thailand • Marshall Cavendish (Malaysia) Sdn Bhd, Times Subang, Lot 46, Subang Hi-Tech Industrial Park, Batu Tiga, 40000 Shah Alam, Selangor Darul Ehsan, Malaysia

Marshall Cavendish is a trademark of Times Publishing Limited

All websites were available and accurate when this book was sent to press.

Library of Congress Cataloging-in-Publication Data
Green, Jen.
Inside animals / by Jen Green.
p. cm. — (Invisible worlds)
"Describes the fascinating animal details that are too small for the unaided eye to see, and how these microscopic systems work to keep the animal alive and healthy"—Provided by publisher.
Includes bibliographical references and index.
ISBN 978-0-7614-4195-3
1. Anatomy—Juvenile literature. 2. Physiology—Juvenile literature.
3. Cells—Juvenile literature. 4. Microorganisms—Juvenile literature. I. Title.
QL806.5.G74 2010
571.1—dc22   2008037241

Series created by The Brown Reference Group Ltd
www.brownreference.com

For The Brown Reference Group Ltd:
Editor: Leon Gray
Designer: Joan Curtis
Picture Managers: Sophie Mortimer and Clare Newman
Picture Researcher: Sean Hannaway
Illustrator: MW Digital Graphics
Managing Editor: Miranda Smith
Design Manager: David Poole
Editorial Director: Lindsey Lowe
Children's Publisher: Anne O'Daly

Consultant: Dr. Christopher Blake

Front cover: Science Photo Library/Dr Gary Gaugler; inset: Shutterstock/Sebastian Knight

The photographs in this book are used by permission and through the courtesy of:
Brown Reference Group: 37 (bottom); Corbis: MIcor Discovery 25 (bottom); FLPA: Image Broker 10, Ron Boardman 17, Malcolm Schuyl 24, Fritz Siedel 34, Martin B. Withers 38, Norbert Wu 35; Photolibrary Group: Roland Birke 4–5; Science Photo Library: George Bernard 37 (top), Dr Jeremy Burgess 20, Scott Camazine and M. Marchaterre 19, Clouds Hill Imaging 14, CNRI 41, Gregory Dimijian 30 (top), Eye of Science 22, Gasto Images 21, Dr Gary Gaugler 44, Steve Gschmeissner 13, 43, Edward Kinsman 27, Microfield Scientific 1, 16, Dr Gopal Murti 8, NIBSC 45, Susumu Nishinaga 30 (bottom), D. Phillips 33, Photo Insolite Realite 42, Peter Scoones 23, Andrew Syred 11, 15, 25 (top), Jerome Wexler 36, Jim Zipp 39; Shutterstock: Arturko 28; Still Pictures: Roland Birke 7.

Printed in Malaysia (T)
1 3 5 6 4 2

# Contents

Introducing the World of Animals . . . . . . . . . . . . . . . .4

Chapter 1: Cells and Body Systems . . . . . . . . . . . . . .6

Chapter 2: Fueling the Body . . . . . . . . . . . . . . . . . .12

Chapter 3: Muscles and Movement . . . . . . . . . . . . .18

Chapter 4: Sensing the World . . . . . . . . . . . . . . . . .26

Chapter 5: Animal Reproduction . . . . . . . . . . . . . . .32

Chapter 6: Pests and Parasites . . . . . . . . . . . . . . . .40

Conclusion . . . . . . . . . . . . . . . . . . . . . . . . . . . . . . .45

Glossary . . . . . . . . . . . . . . . . . . . . . . . . . . . . . . . . .46

Find Out More . . . . . . . . . . . . . . . . . . . . . . . . . . . .47

Index . . . . . . . . . . . . . . . . . . . . . . . . . . . . . . . . . . .48

# Introducing the World of Animals

From the largest elephants on the land to the microscopic insect larvae in the oceans, animals share features that set them apart from other types of living things, such as plants. All animals breathe and can move at least part of their bodies. Some have senses such as vision and hearing to tell them about their surroundings. Animals feed and get rid of waste so that they can grow and develop. In the 1600s, scientists started to study the anatomy, or structure, of animals using microscopes. Scientists now use extremely powerful microscopes to look at animals in great detail and learn about them.

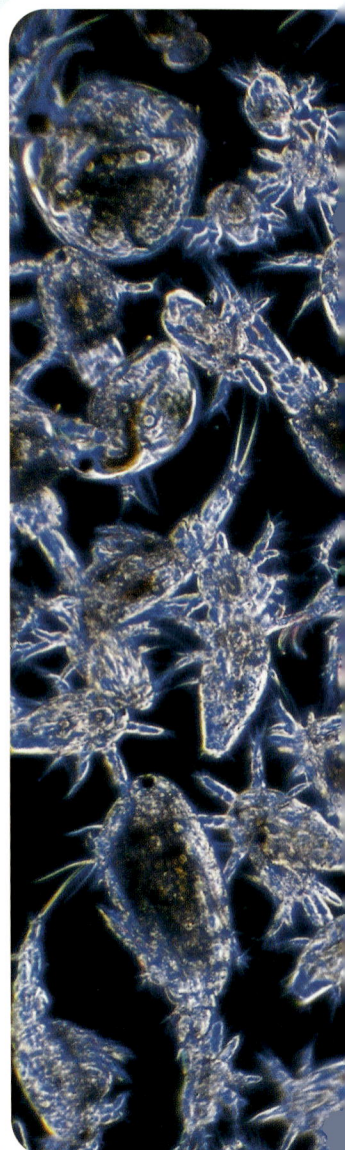

These tiny animals are water fleas and their larvae. Gradually, the smaller larvae will develop into the larger adult water fleas.

# CHAPTER 1

# Cells and Body Systems

Animals come in many different shapes and sizes. Some, such as zooplankton, are smaller than the period at the end of this sentence. Some whales are bigger than an airplane. Despite these differences, zooplankton and whales are part of the animal kingdom.

All animals are made up of tiny units called **cells**. These miniature structures fit together to form the body of the animal. Extremely small animals, such as rotifers, are made up of just a few cells. Experts call these creatures "simple" animals. Larger, more complex animals, such as humans, are made up of billions of cells. Stretched out in a line, one billion average-size cells would be 6.25 miles (10 kilometers) long.

Other living things, such as plants, also consist of cells, but they are built differently from animals. Plant cells have a rigid outer wall. Because animal cells do not have this hard cell wall, they are more flexible. A softer layer, called a **membrane**, surrounds the animal cell. Plant cells also contain a green chemical, called chlorophyll, which enables them to make their own food from the Sun. Animal cells do not contain chlorophyll and so they must eat food to stay alive.

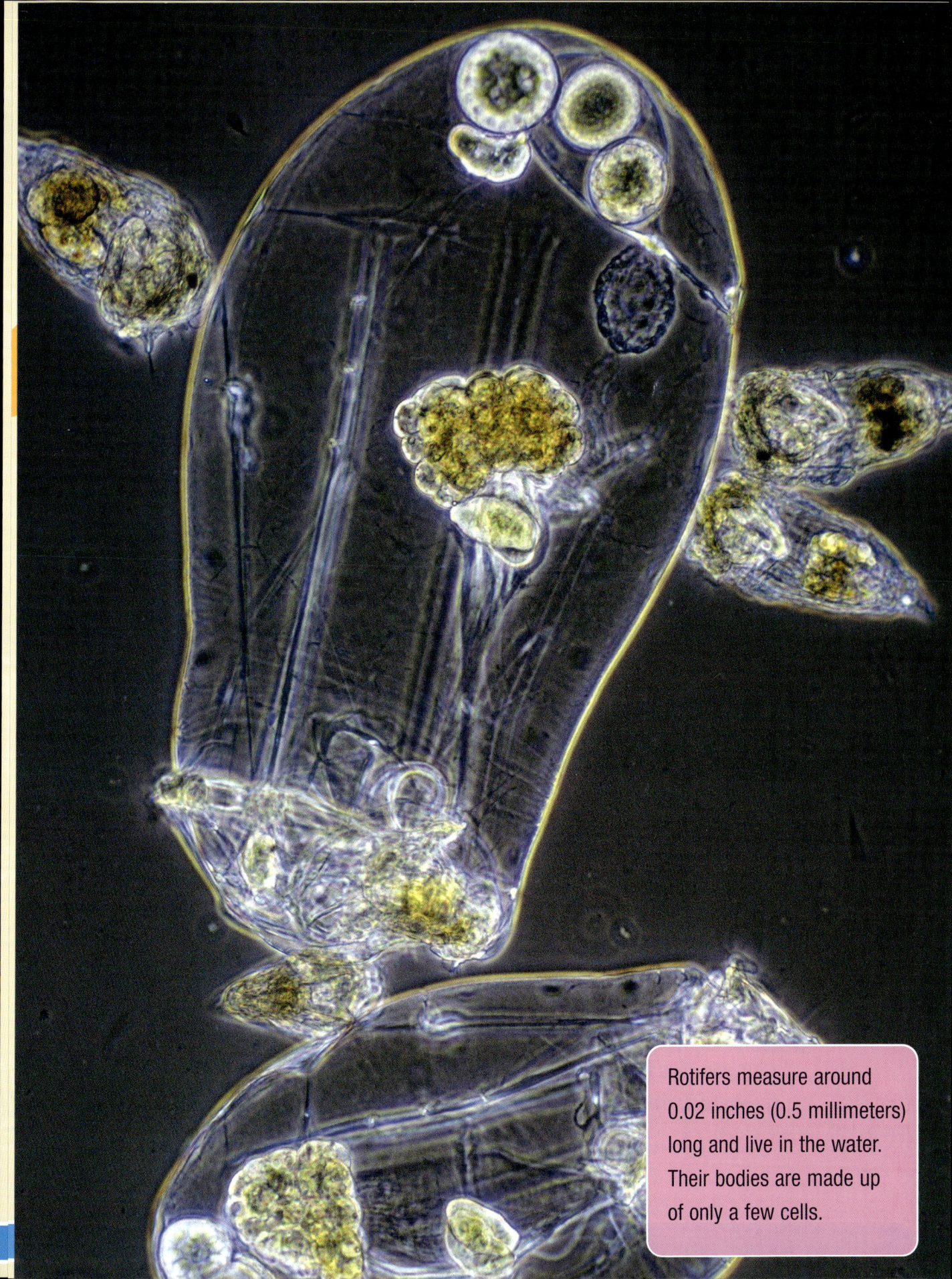

Rotifers measure around 0.02 inches (0.5 millimeters) long and live in the water. Their bodies are made up of only a few cells.

## CHAPTER 2

# Fueling the Body

Food is the fuel for every living thing. It provides the energy needed to keep cells working properly. Plants can make their own food. The green leaves of plants make food by trapping the energy from sunlight. Animals cannot do this. They get energy they need through two main body processes: breathing and **digestion**. Breathing helps an animal take in oxygen. Digestion helps an animal to break down food into smaller substances so the body can absorb the energy from it. Both of these essential life processes take place inside the invisible world of cells.

Cells in an animal's body use oxygen to unlock the energy in food. Land animals breathe in oxygen from the air. Underwater animals can take in oxygen from the water.

Oxygen and nutrients travel around an animal's body in blood. In simple animals, the blood flows freely around the body. In complex animals, the blood moves around a circulatory system. This system consists of a muscular pump called the heart, a network of tubes called blood vessels, and the blood itself. The heart pumps blood through blood vessels to every cell in the animal's body.

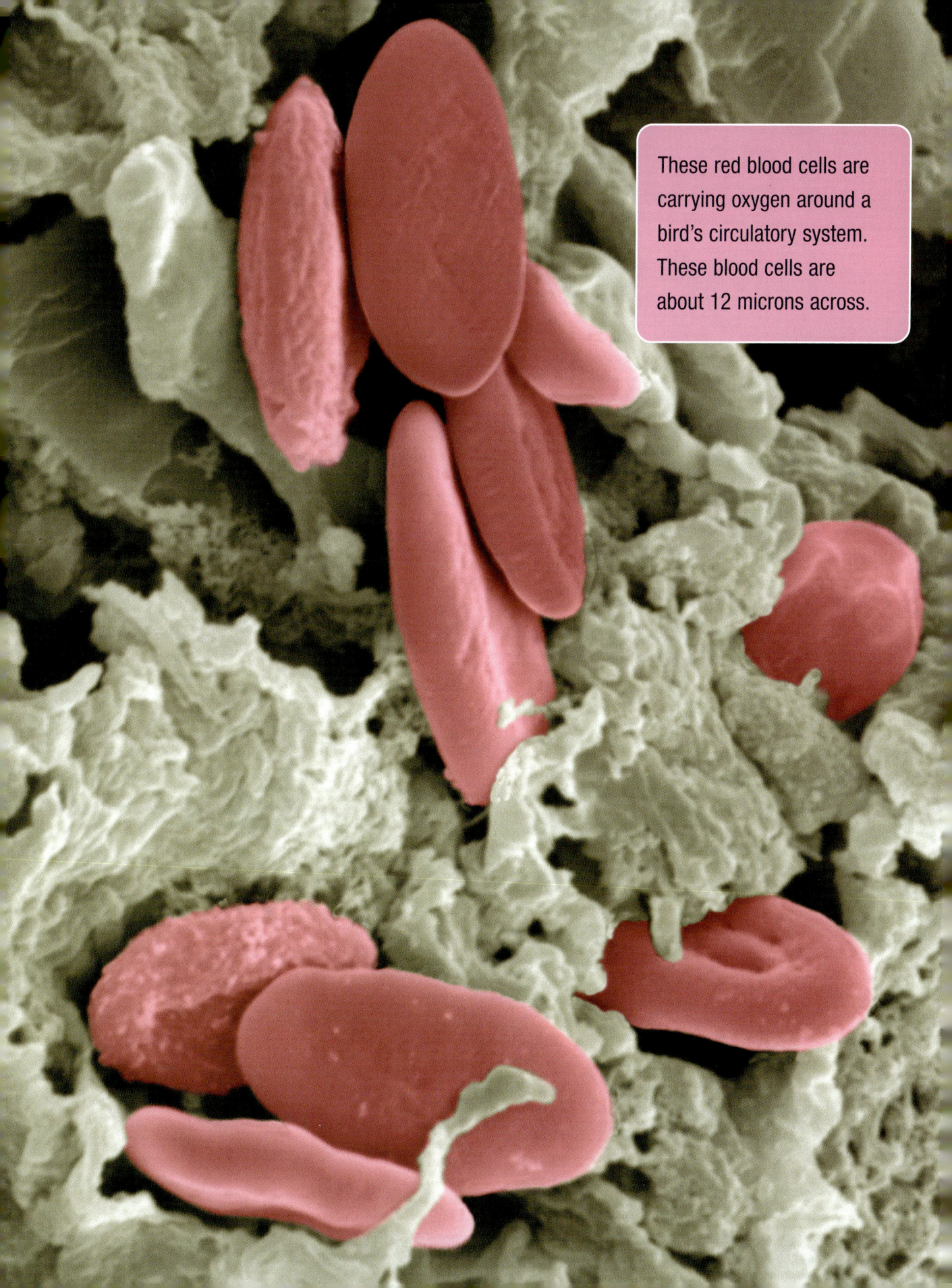

These red blood cells are carrying oxygen around a bird's circulatory system. These blood cells are about 12 microns across.

Inside Animals

# Feeding and Digestion

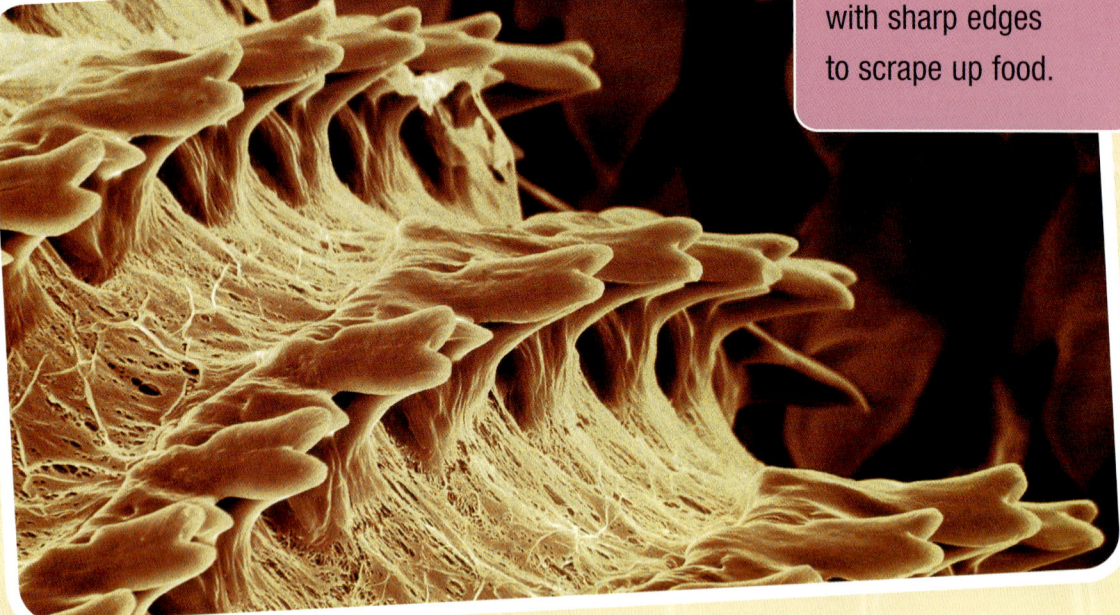

This image shows the rasping tongue, or radula, of a snail (magnified seven thousand times.) The radula is covered with sharp edges to scrape up food.

### ? Did You Know?

Whales are some of the largest of all animals, but many eat some of the smallest. Filter-feeding whales sieve shrimplike animals out of the water using bony plates inside their mouths.

Animals can be divided into three main groups based on what they eat. One big group is the herbivores or plant-eaters. Plants, such as grasses, are hard to digest, so herbivores use up a lot of energy breaking down their food. As a result, they need to eat more plant food to get all the nutrients they need. Another big group is the carnivores or meat-eaters. Many meat-eaters are

# Fueling the Body

predators. They catch their prey using body parts such as sharp claws and teeth, or poisonous chemicals. The third group is the omnivores. These animals eat both plants and animals. This group includes bears, pigs, and humans.

## Digestion

An animal needs to digest its food to break it down into small molecules and absorb it into the body. Simple single-celled animals do not have digestive systems. They surround their food and simply absorb it into the cell. Larger, more complex animals may have digestive systems that include mouthparts, such as a beak or jaws with teeth, a stomach, and intestines. Plant-eaters such as cows have four stomachs to break down their tough, stringy food.

### Close up

Most flies need to liquify their food to eat it. They do this by squirting saliva onto the food to dissolve it. The flies then suck up the liquid using their mouthparts (the labium and labrum), which are shaped like a spongy pad.

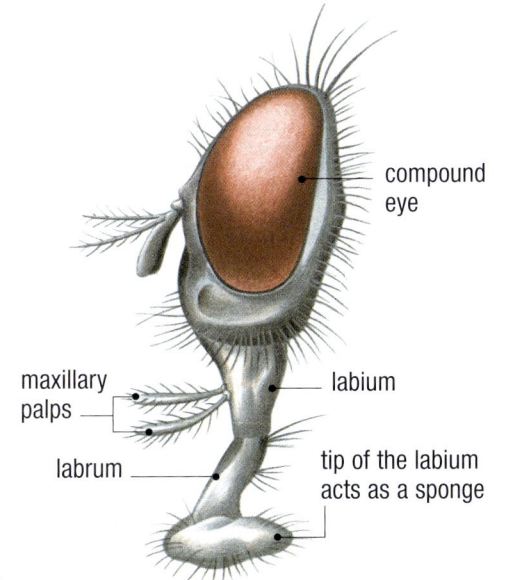

A powerful microscope has captured this image of the head and mouthparts of a fruit fly.

Inside Animals

# Breathing

Animals need oxygen to survive. Inside cells, oxygen combines with food molecules to release energy. This process is called cell **respiration**. In simple animals, oxygen seeps into the body directly, and waste gases seep out. Large animals, such as birds, fish, and mammals, breathe in oxygen using gills or lungs.

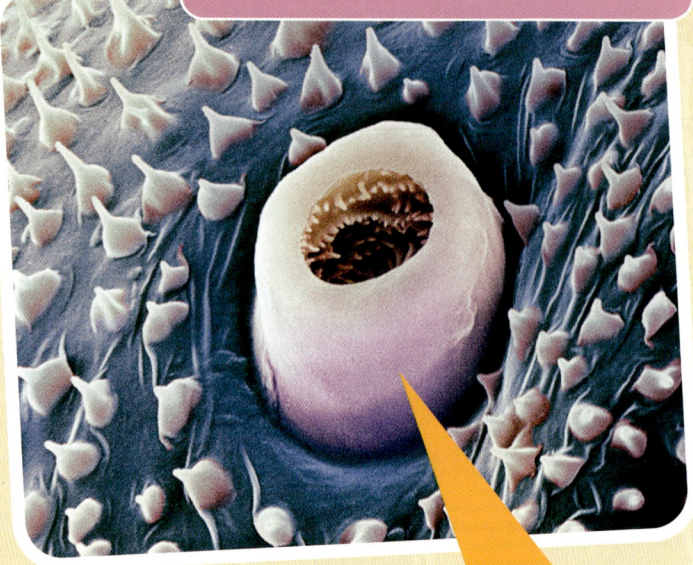

A powerful microscope captures an image of the spiracle of a garden tiger moth caterpillar.

## Close Up

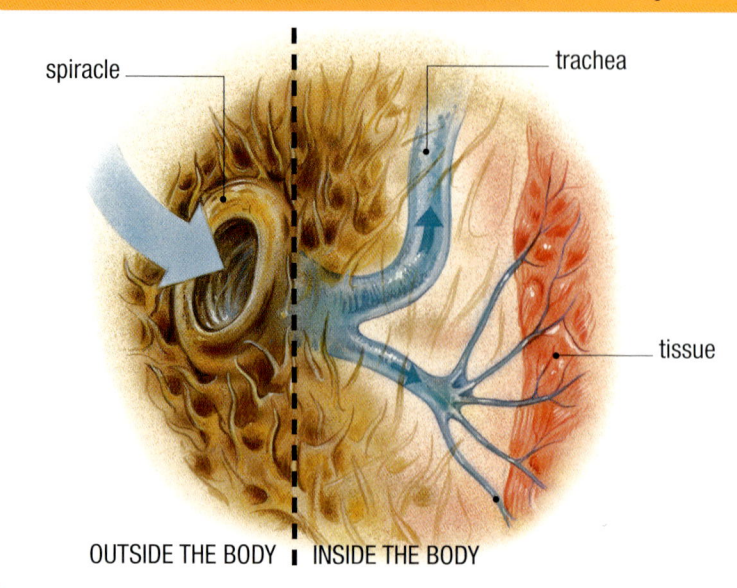

spiracle — trachea — tissue

OUTSIDE THE BODY | INSIDE THE BODY

An insect absorbs oxygen from the air through tiny openings called spiracles. The spiracles are located along the insect's body. They lead to tubes called tracheae that carry oxygen inside the insect's body.

16

# Fueling the Body

This photo shows the gill filaments of a salmon. The fish absorbs oxygen from water using branching structures inside its gills.

 **Did You Know?**

Amphibians, such as frogs, live both on land and in the water. They have lungs to absorb oxygen from air. They can also absorb oxygen from water through their skin.

## Breathing in air

Land-dwelling animals take in oxygen from the air through their lungs. In mammals, the air passes into the lungs, where a network of fine tubes lead to tiny air sacs called **alveoli**. The alveoli are surrounded by a network of blood vessels called capillaries. Oxygen seeps through the capillary walls and into the blood. At the same time, waste products such as carbon dioxide gas pass out of the capillaries and into the lungs to be breathed out.

## Breathing in water

Fish absorb oxygen in water using their gills. Water passes in through the fish's mouth and out over the gills. Feathery structures in the gills absorb oxygen into the blood, while waste carbon dioxide passes out.

### Fast Facts

- Whales can hold their breath for over an hour when they dive.

- Sharks have to keep swimming to keep water flowing over their gills so they can breathe.

# CHAPTER 3
# Muscles and Movement

Animals move around from place to place to find food, to escape predators, and to reproduce. Different animals move in different ways. How an animal moves depends on the shape of its body and where it lives.

Many animals live on land. Most of them have legs that they use to climb, crawl, or walk. Animals such as snakes and worms slide over the ground. Other animals have wings that enable them to fly in the air. Some animals live in water and have fins and flippers to help them swim.

Animals move by contracting and relaxing their muscles. The muscles are made of bundles of long strands, called muscle fibers. Muscle fibers are made from even finer strands called filaments. These long strings of cells stretch in one direction to help the animal move.

The brain is the control center of the animal's body. It controls the movement of the animal. When an animal wants to move, the brain sends signals to the muscles through a network of branching fibers called **nerves**. The nerves stimulate muscle fibers, which contract and pull on the bone to which they are attached. This causes the movement.

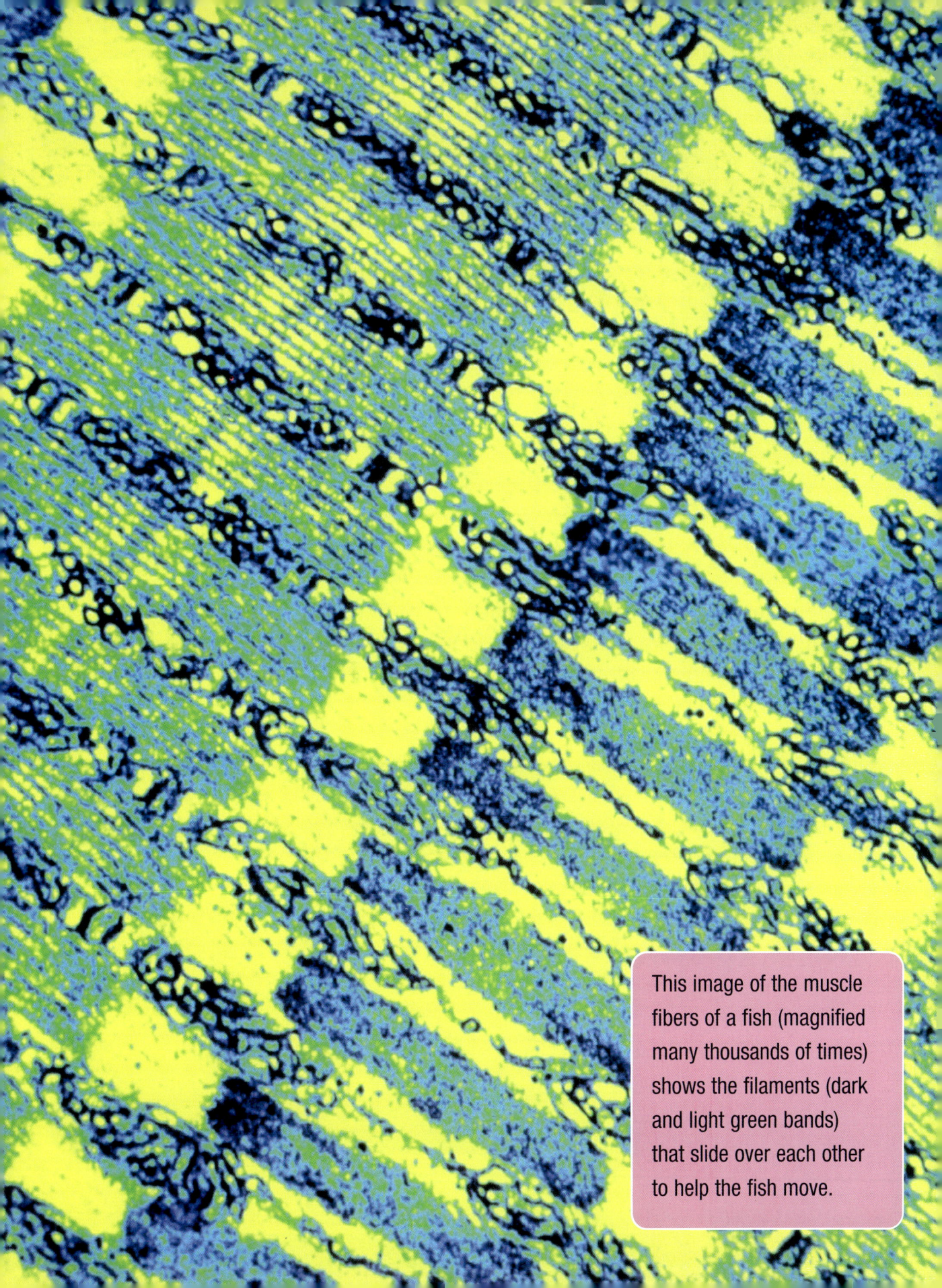

This image of the muscle fibers of a fish (magnified many thousands of times) shows the filaments (dark and light green bands) that slide over each other to help the fish move.

Inside Animals

# Running, Crawling, and Leaping

Animals that live on land have bodies that allow them to crawl, hop, run, or slither. Most land animals that have a backbone, such as birds, frogs, lizards, and mammals, share a similar body design. They have four limbs and usually run on all fours. The front limbs of a bird are its wings, but it uses its back limbs to move over the ground. A few mammals, such as humans and kangaroos, also move on their back limbs.

### Did You Know?

Fleas are fantastic jumpers. These insects can leap up to 130 times their own height. If you could jump as high as a flea, you would be able to jump over a multistory building!

These are the tiny hairlike tubes that cover the footpad of a fly. The tubes release a sticky substance that helps the fly stick to surfaces.

20

# Muscles and Movement

An ant has three pairs of legs that attach to its middle body segment, which is called the thorax. The ant raises and lowers each leg in order to move along the ground.

## Close Up

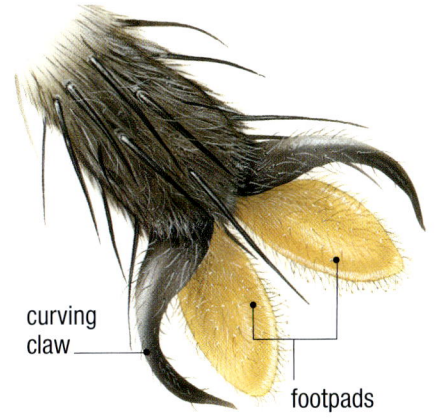

curving claw

footpads

A housefly has two curving claws on each foot. Tiny tubes cover the spongy footpads between the claws. The tubes release a sticky substance that allows the fly to climb up windows and even walk across the ceiling.

## Moving on many legs

Insects have three pairs of legs. As they run, the front and back legs on one side touch the ground with the middle leg on the other side. Then these three legs are raised, while the others touch the ground. Centipedes and millipedes have many pairs of legs. As they run, the legs move in waves, one after the other.

## Moving without legs

Worms and snakes move without any legs. Worms move forward by lengthening and shortening sections of their bodies. Snakes throw their bodies into S-shaped curves that push against the ground.

# Inside Animals

# Swimming and Floating

Animals that live underwater have bodies suited to moving in watery places. Scientists divide aquatic animals into three groups. Free swimmers, such as fish and whales, actively swim in the water. Drifters such as jellyfish are usually carried along in water currents. The third group includes animals, such as crabs and starfish, that creep along the riverbed or ocean floor.

## Tails, fins, and flippers

Crocodiles and fish swim by swishing their tails from side to side. Powerful muscles hidden inside the bodies of these animals propel them through the water.

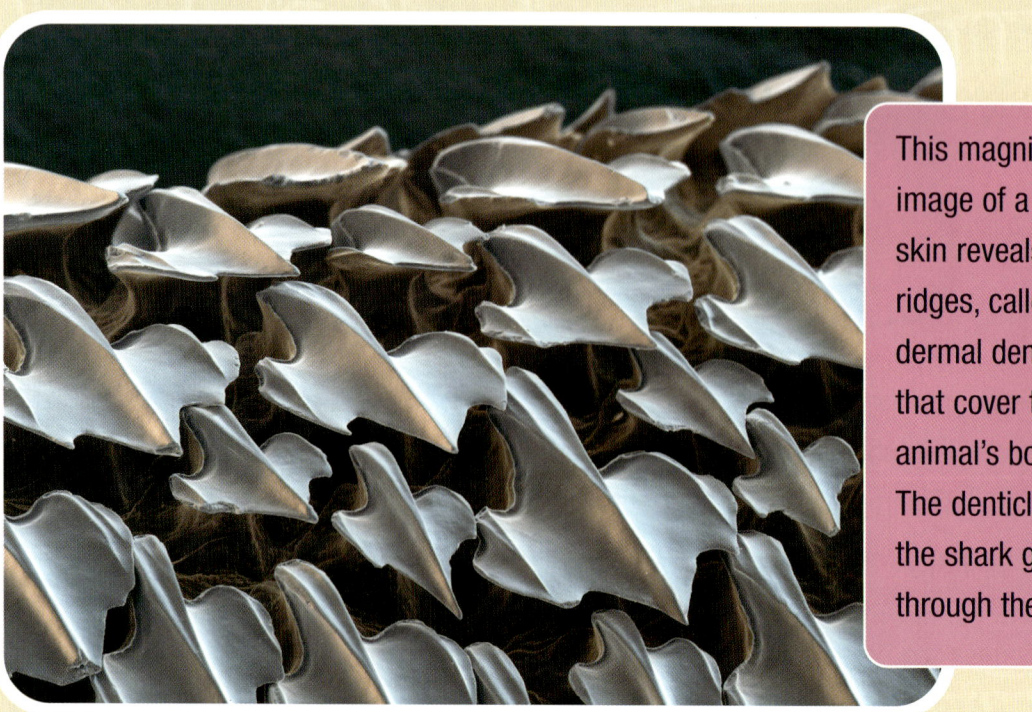

This magnified image of a shark's skin reveals tiny ridges, called dermal denticles, that cover the animal's body. The denticles help the shark glide through the water

22

# Muscles and Movement

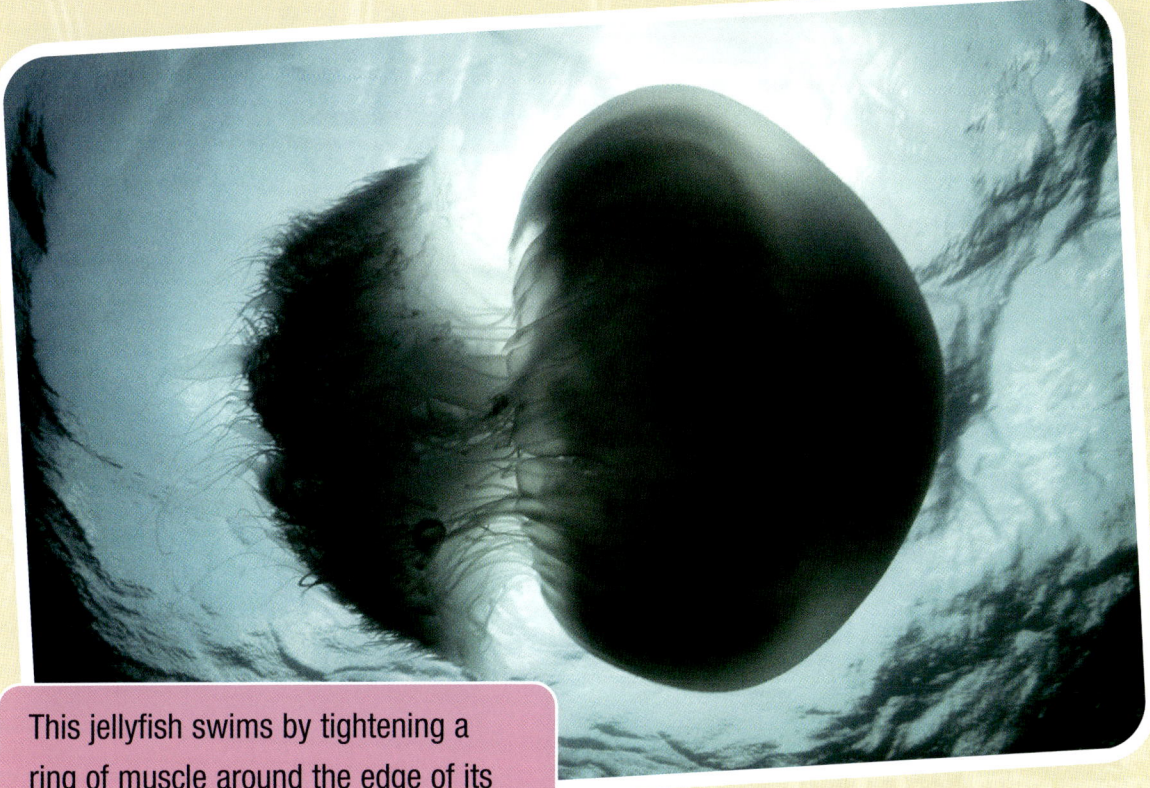

This jellyfish swims by tightening a ring of muscle around the edge of its bell-shaped body. As the water squirts backward, the animal shoots forward.

Fish use fins on their bodies to steer and keep steady. Dolphins and whales beat their tails up and down. They steer using their front flippers as paddles. The bodies of all these free swimmers have streamlined shapes to glide through the water.

## Drifting along

Large numbers of animals float freely in rivers and oceans, carried along in the currents. They range in size from microscopic insect larvae to the 50-foot (15-meter) long Portuguese man-of-war.

### Did You Know?

Octopus and squid swim by squirting a jet of water out of a funnel, called a siphon. This siphon is located underneath their baglike bodies.

23

# Inside Animals

# Flying and Gliding

A hummingbird looks as if it is hovering without moving, but its wings are beating about 80 times every second. The wing beat is far too fast for humans to see.

Bats, birds, and insects, are the only animals that can fly. Flying allows them to escape from their enemies and reach food that other animals cannot reach. Some flying animals make a long journey, or migration, to reach a safe place to breed.

## Birds and bats

From the side, a bird's wing is shaped in a way that helps the bird rise through the air as it flaps its wings. Feathers give the bird the control it needs to steer, glide, take off, and land. A bat's wings are

## Fast Facts

- Gliding animals "fly" on invisible air currents using winglike body parts, such as flaps of skin between the arms and legs, to slow their descent.

- The bumblebee bat is the world's smallest flying vertebrate. It weighs 0.07 ounces (2 grams) and measures 1.1 inches (30 millimeters) in length.

## Muscles and Movement

### Close up

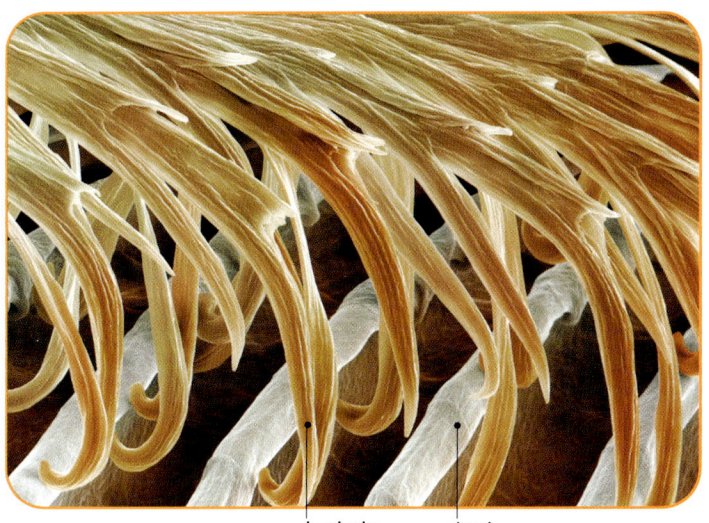

barbule   barb

A feather consists of a central shaft and hundreds of parallel vanes, which branch out from the shaft. Each vane is formed by a barb. Tiny barbules stick out of the barb and hook onto the barb of the next vane. This binds the barbs to form a strong sheet.

simply flaps of skin that stretch over the bat's long finger-bones.

### Flying insects

Insects have one or two pairs of wings. These are attached to the insect's middle section, or thorax. The wings flip up and down as muscles pull on the roof and sides of the thorax. A butterfly's front and back wings move together. A dragonfly's two sets of wings move independently, which allows it to hover in midair.

The wings of a butterfly are covered with tiny, overlapping scales. The scales give the wings their bright colors and patterns.

25

# CHAPTER 4

# Sensing the World

An animal's senses tell it about the world in which it lives. Animals use senses such as sight and smell so they can find their way around, escape predators, track down food, and find a mate.

In simple animals such as hydras, jellyfish, and starfish, the sensory system consists of a network of nerves, called a nerve net, that spreads throughout the animal's body. The nerves transmit electrical signals around the network in a similar way to the electrical wires in a computer. In complex animals, such as vertebrates, the sensory system includes a brain and spinal cord, as well as a network of nerve fibers and nerve cells.

An animal's senses are made of sensitive cells called receptors. In senses such as sight, these cells group to form organs such as the eye. Sense receptors flash signals to the brain through the nerves. The brain makes sense of the signals.

Most animals have the same five senses as humans have. They are sight, hearing, smell, taste, and touch. Some animals also have extra senses. The senses of some animals are suited to being diurnal (active during the day). Others have senses suited to being nocturnal (active at night).

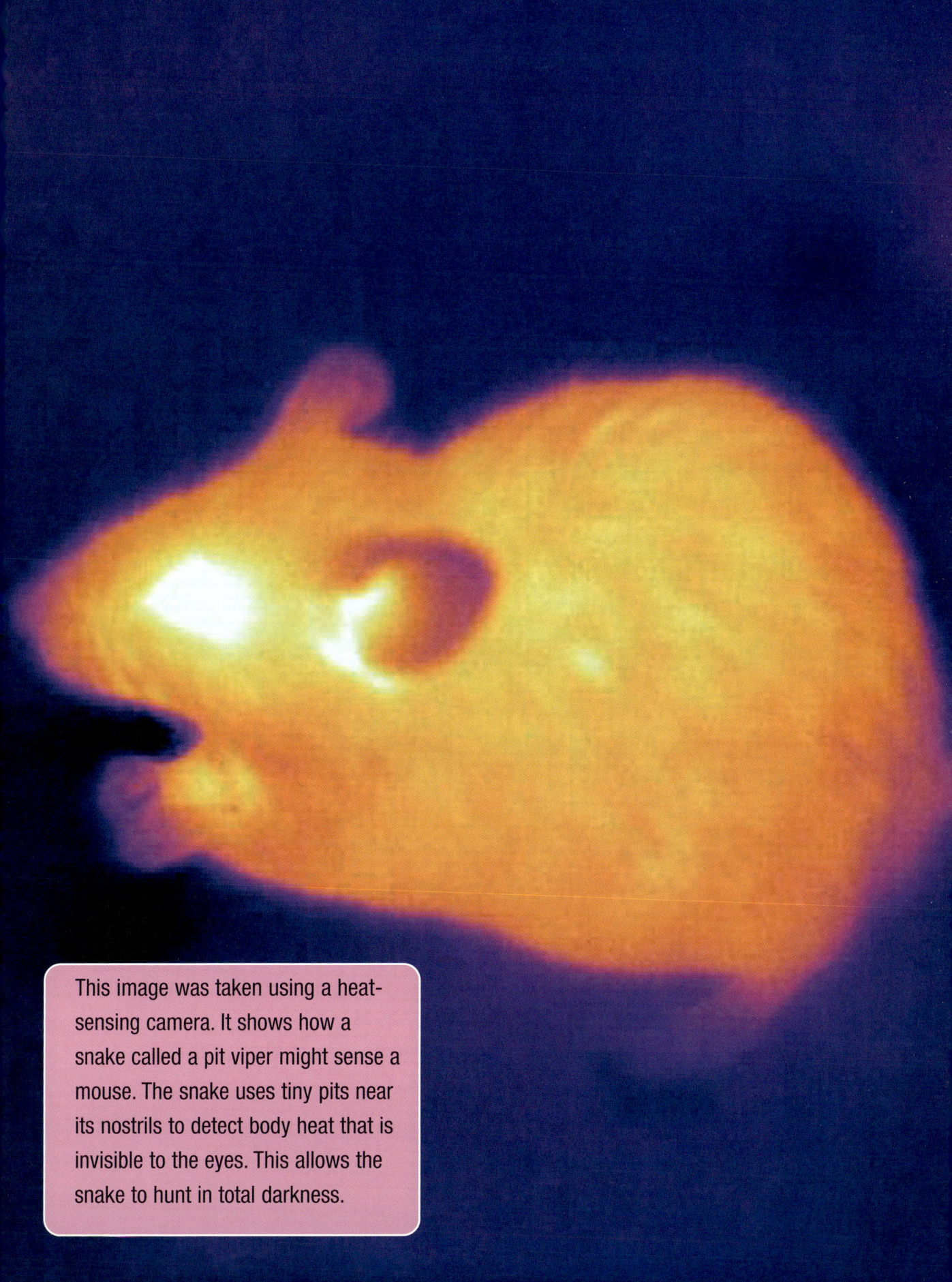

This image was taken using a heat-sensing camera. It shows how a snake called a pit viper might sense a mouse. The snake uses tiny pits near its nostrils to detect body heat that is invisible to the eyes. This allows the snake to hunt in total darkness.

Inside Animals

# Sight and Hearing

Sight is a very important sense for humans, but animals such as hawks can see in far more detail than people can. Insects such as dragonflies can see a type of light called ultraviolet light, which is invisible to humans.

## Seeing at night

Nocturnal animals have a layer of reflective cells at the

The eyes of this dragonfly cover much of the insect's head, giving the insect good all-round vision.

## Close up

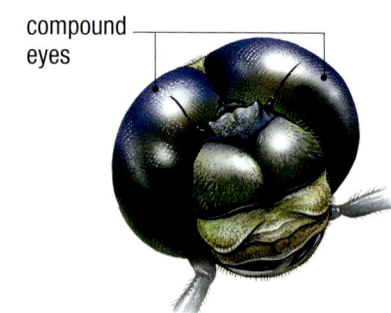

compound eyes

The eyes of a dragonfly are called compound eyes. Each eye may be made up of thousands of individual lenses. Each lens produces a tiny image of the object in view, which then forms part of a bigger picture.

# Sensing the World

## Fast Facts

- Bees have more than 5,000 tiny lenses in each eye.

- Many spiders have eight eyes. Spiders use their eyes to judge distance, helping these predators catch their prey.

## Hearing

Most animals hear using ears. The main part of the ear is inside the head. A membrane called the ear drum vibrates to the sound waves passing through the air or water. This sends signals to the brain.

## Sensing with sound

Dolphins and bats use echolocation to sense their surroundings. They emit a stream of high-pitched squeaks or clicks and listen for the echoes that bounce back off prey.

back of their eyes. These cells allow the animals to see in very dim light. Other nocturnal hunters have huge eyes. Some animals that live in the darkness, such as cave crickets, have no eyes at all.

This illustration shows how a dolphin makes and receives echolocation signals to sense its surroundings and locate food.

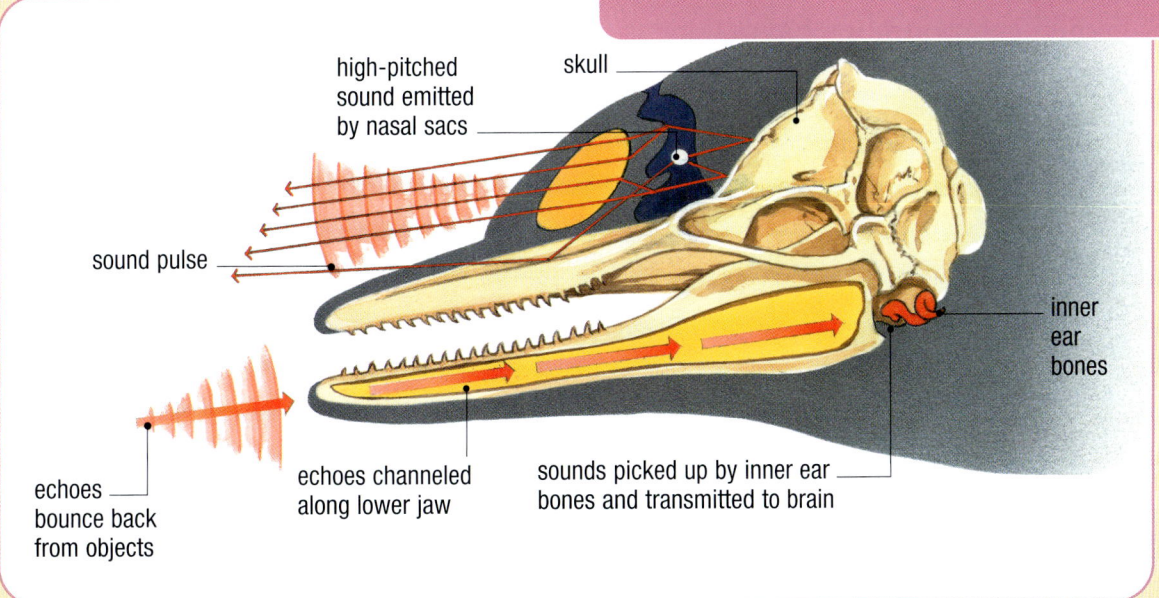

high-pitched sound emitted by nasal sacs

skull

sound pulse

inner ear bones

echoes bounce back from objects

echoes channeled along lower jaw

sounds picked up by inner ear bones and transmitted to brain

Inside Animals

# Scent, Taste, and Touch

Many animals do not rely on vision to make sense of the world. Instead, they use invisible clues such as scents, tastes, and touch to build up a picture of their surroundings.

## Scent and taste

Animals such as dogs, sharks, and many insects have a keener sense of smell than humans have. Insects use their long antennae to feel and gather scents and tastes. The male atlas moth can use its antennae to pick up the scent of a female moth that may be several miles away.

A pit viper flicks out its forked tongue to pick up scent molecules in the air.

A moth's antenna is covered with sensory hairs that detect movement and smell.

## Touch

Touch is vital to many animals that hunt at night or in murky water. Many animals, such as cats, mice, and walruses, have long, sensitive whiskers on

# Sensing the World

## Close up

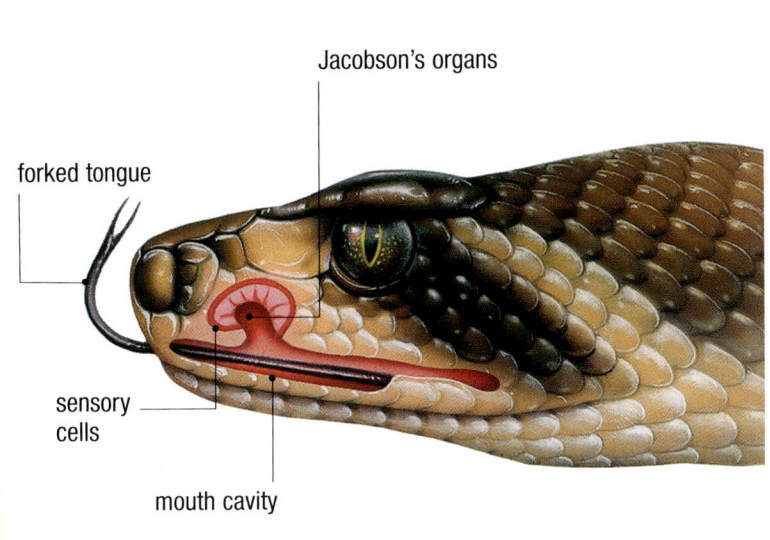

- forked tongue
- Jacobson's organs
- sensory cells
- mouth cavity

A snake smells and tastes using its forked tongue, which flickers in and out to gather scent molecules in the air. When a snake brings in its tongue, it touches two tiny pits, or Jacobson's organs, in the roof of its mouth. These send signals to the brain.

their snouts. These help them to find food and avoid bumping into things. Some animals have sensitive hairs all over their bodies to feel their way around.

## Underwater senses

Squid and sea anemones have long tentacles to find and seize prey. Most fish have a sensory line, called the lateral line, that runs along the side of their bodies. The lateral line picks up vibrations, or tiny ripples, in the water, that are made by moving objects such as prey.

## Fast Facts

- A dog's nose is so good at detecting smells that some are used to sniff out hidden drugs and explosives.

- Some insects have sense organs in unusual places. For example, houseflies taste with their feet!

- A star-nosed mole uses the ring of tentacles on its nose to feel for prey such as worms.

# CHAPTER 5

# Animal Reproduction

Reproduction is the process of producing new life. Animals reproduce to ensure that the **species** as a whole will survive to the next generation. A species is a particular kind of animal that can only mate with an animal of the same kind, but of the opposite sex. Mating means that a male and a female come together during a process called sex.

At the microscopic level, sex is when the male's sex cell, or **sperm,** joins up with the female's sex cell, or egg. Sex cells carry **genes,** which are instructions that make up every living **organism**. Genes are found in the center, or nuclei, of cells.

The genes from the male join in new combinations with the genes from a female to create a new animal. This means that the young animal has similar, but slightly different, features to both of its parents. So the young might have the same genes for eye or hair color because its parents have passed on the gene for eye and hair color.

In some cases, animals reproduce without mating. This is known as asexual reproduction. When this happens, the young animals are identical copies of their parents. Asexual reproduction is more common with simple animals such as jellyfish and hydras.

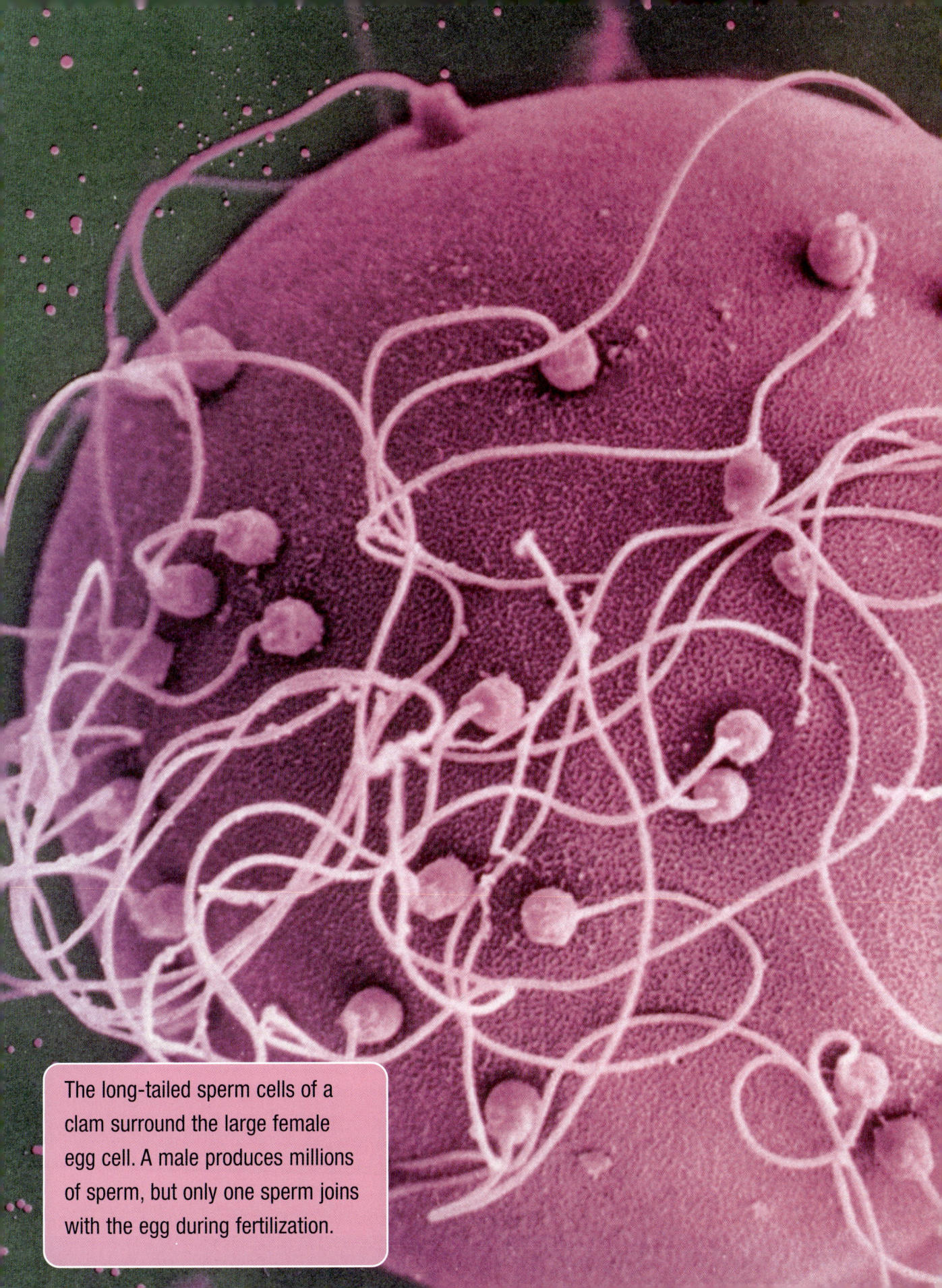

The long-tailed sperm cells of a clam surround the large female egg cell. A male produces millions of sperm, but only one sperm joins with the egg during fertilization.

Inside Animals

# Reproduction without Mating

This image shows an animal called a hydra reproducing in a process that is known as budding.

When animals reproduce without mating, the offspring are identical to their parents. They are called **clones**. One of the main advantages of asexual reproduction is that an animal does not need to find a mate with which to breed. However, any weakness in the parent will be passed on to the young.

## Fragmentation

Some animals reproduce by simply breaking off part of their bodies. Each part develops into a new adult.

## Animal Reproduction

This starfish has lost an arm (bottom), but the tip is being regenerated.

### ? Did You Know?

Some animals can lose body parts that may grow back as cells divide to take their place. If a predator bites off the arm of a starfish, the starfish can grow a new arm. The arm may even develop into a new starfish. Some lizards can grow a new tail if it is bitten off by a predator.

This type of asexual reproduction is called fragmentation. Sea stars, annelid worms such as earthworms, and sponges reproduce in this way.

### Fast Facts

- Some flatworms reproduce by splitting in two and growing into two new flatworms.

- After splitting, special cells in the bodies of the flatworms grow into different types of cells.

## Budding

Sea anemones and tiny water animals called hydras reproduce by budding. A growth, called a bud, appears on one side of the animal. The bud swells and separates from the parent to form a new animal.

## Parthenogensis

Sometimes a female egg will develop into a new animal without being fertilized by a male sperm. This is called **parthenogenesis**, and it is found in some insects, such as aphids, and a few vertebrates, such as frogs and lizards.

35

Inside Animals

# Sexual Reproduction

In most complex animals, a male and female pair up to breed. This is known as sexual reproduction. The sperm from the male animal joins with the egg of the female animal in a process called **fertilization**. In fish, frogs, and other aquatic animals, fertilization usually takes place in water. In other animals, it takes place inside the female. The fertilized egg cell begins to divide again and again, forming a ball of cells that develops into the young.

## Eggs or living young?

In animals such as fish, frogs, birds and reptiles, breeding almost always involves laying eggs. These may be

This photograph shows a chick developing inside an egg. The chick has formed from a single fertilized egg cell.

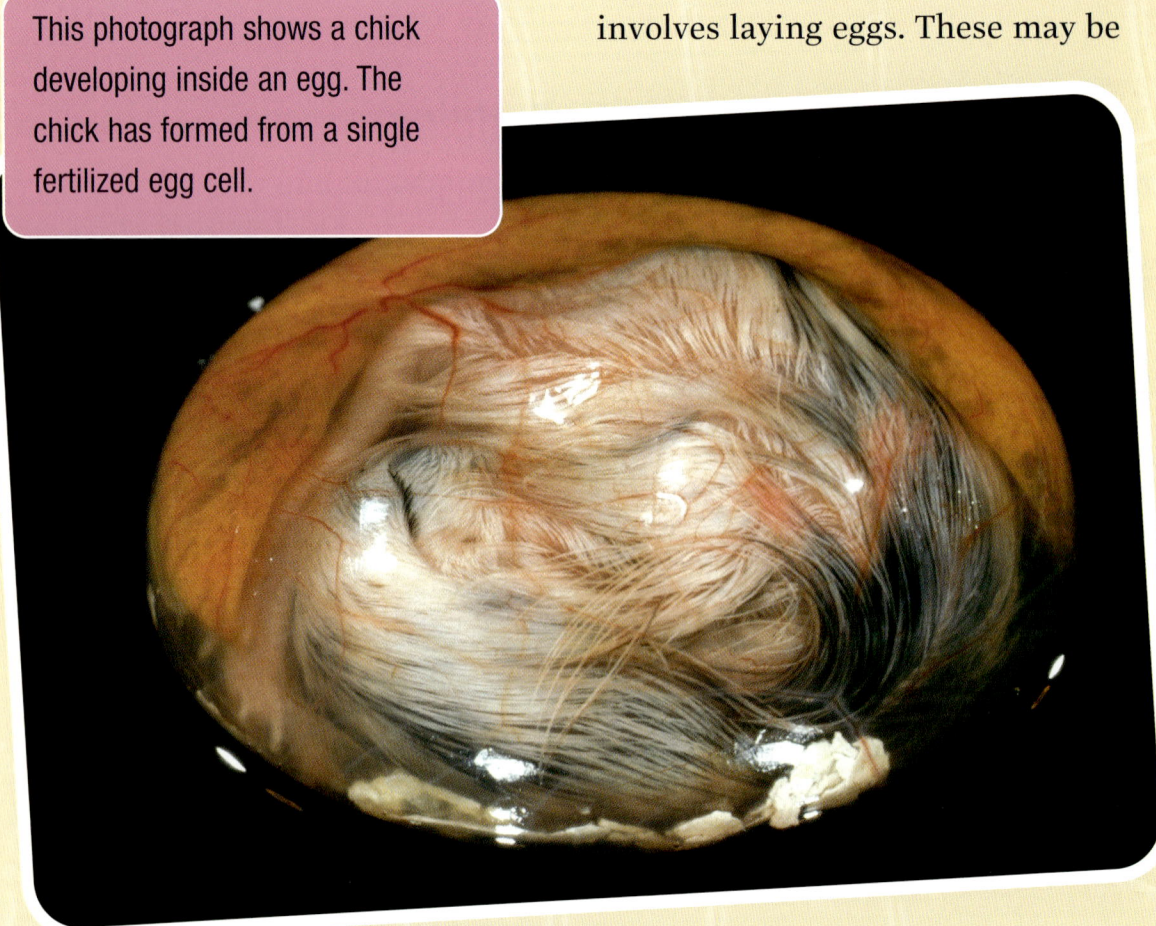

# Animal Reproduction

hard-shelled like chickens' eggs or soft like frog eggs. The developing young are hidden away inside the egg until they are ready to hatch. The eggs of most mammals develop inside the females. The young are hidden away inside the female's body and grow and develop until they are ready to be born.

## ? Did You Know?

The largest cell in the human body is the female egg cell. It is about 120 microns across. The male sperm is the smallest cell in the human body. A sperm cell is about 4 microns long, excluding the tail.

## Both male and female

Most animals are either male or female, but snails can produce both male and female sex cells. They are known as **hermaphrodites**. When two snails meet they swap male sex cells to fertilize each other's eggs. Both snails then produce young.

## Aphid clones

Aphids are unusual because they can breed both sexually and asexually. In the spring, females that have hatched from eggs reproduce by making clones of themselves. In the fall, male and female aphids mate. The females then lay eggs that will hatch into new aphids the following spring.

A female aphid gives birth to a clone formed by asexual reproduction. The two aphids are genetically identical.

Inside Animals

# Metamorphosis

Some young animals that hatch from eggs look nothing like their parents. As they grow into adults, they pass through an amazing transformation called complete **metamorphosis**. The word *metamorphosis* means "change."

## Complete metamorphosis

After mating, the female butterfly lays eggs. The young hatch out as wingless caterpillars that look completely different from the adults. When the caterpillar has fully grown, it enters a new stage in its life. It becomes a pupa. Inside the hard case of the pupa, the caterpillar's

### ? Did You Know?

Animal life spans vary. Many insects live for just a few weeks or months. Small mammals such as rats live about four years. Elephants live for up to 75 years. Some tortoises can live for 120 years.

After mating, a female frog lays hundreds of eggs, called spawn, in the water. The fertilized cell develops inside each egg, and a tadpole eventually emerges.

38

# Animal Reproduction

body breaks down and is rebuilt. After a few days, an adult butterfly emerges from the case.

## Incomplete metamorphosis

A newly hatched grasshopper looks like its parents, but it is small and wingless. As the grasshopper grows, it sheds its hard outer case several times. Each time, it emerges in a bigger case with space in which to grow. Eventually, the wings form, and it becomes an adult. This process of gradual change is called incomplete metamorphosis.

A monarch butterfly emerges from a pupa as a winged adult.

## Close up

adult frogs mate
tadpole frog
legs appear
eggs
tadpole emerges

Frogs undergo complete metamorphosis. They hatch from eggs laid in the water. The legless tadpoles that emerge swim using their long tails. As the tadpole grows, tiny legs appear, and the tail shrinks. Eventually a tiny frog climbs out of the water.

39

# CHAPTER 6

# Pests and Parasites

**P**arasites live on or inside the bodies of animals. The parasite steals valuable nutrients from the **host** animal, for example, by drinking its blood. Some parasites are very small and hard to see. They include single-celled bacteria and particles called viruses. Other parasites are animals and include fleas, mites, mosquitoes, tapeworms, and ticks. These parasites live on a range of host animals, such as cats, dogs, and even humans.

Parasites, such as fleas and lice, live on the bodies of their hosts, for example, in the skin and hair. Others, such as tapeworms, live in the warm, damp insides of the host. Some parasites, such as blood-sucking leeches, spend only a short time on the host, while others stay for longer. Some tiny parasites even live on the bodies of other parasites.

Most parasites live on their hosts without killing them. If the host dies, they would have to find a new source of food. But some parasites carry diseases that can kill humans and animals. One of the world's deadliest human diseases is malaria. Malaria spreads when mosquitoes bite humans and drink their blood. As mosquitoes feed, tiny organisms enter the blood and cause malaria.

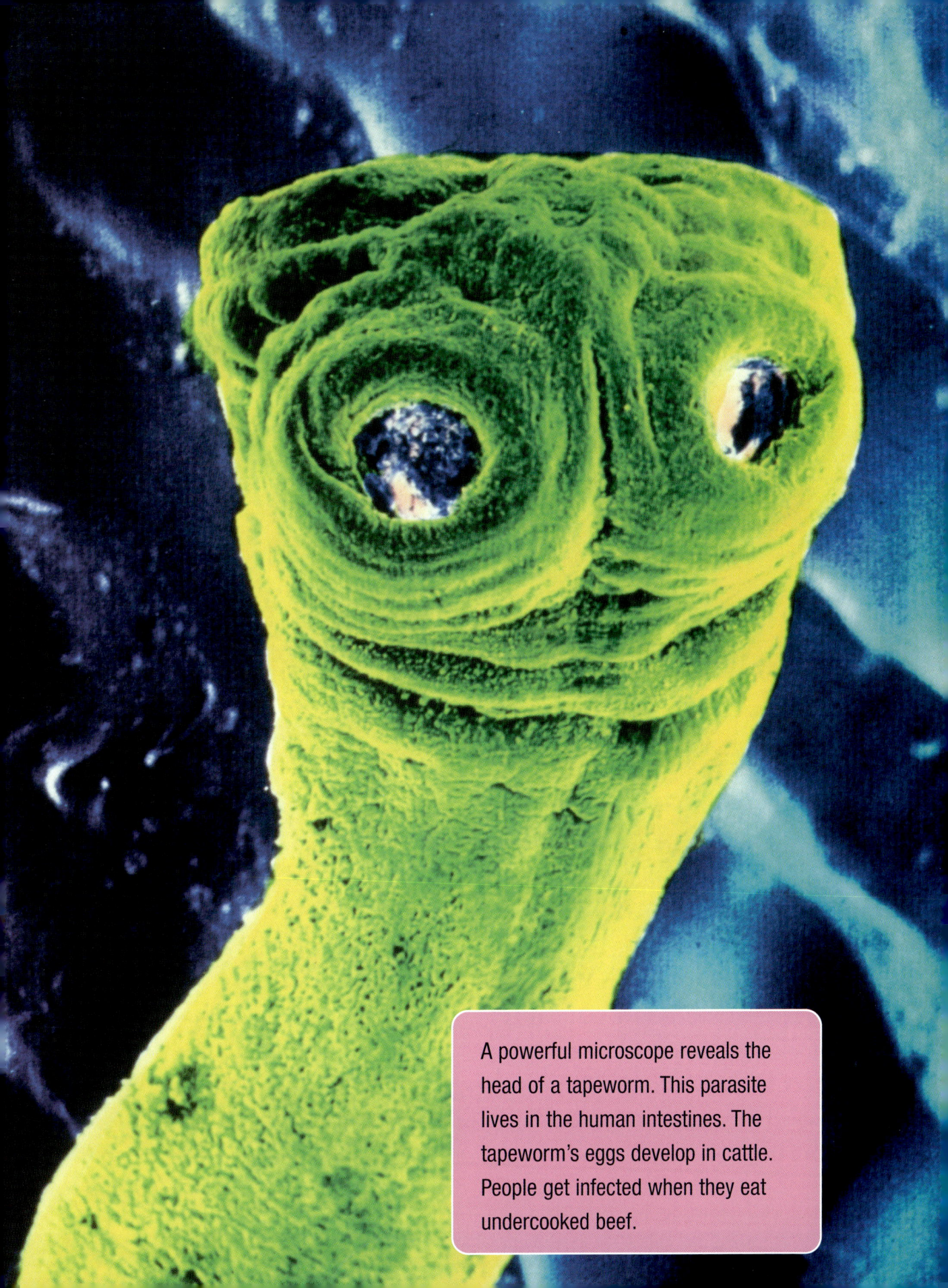

A powerful microscope reveals the head of a tapeworm. This parasite lives in the human intestines. The tapeworm's eggs develop in cattle. People get infected when they eat undercooked beef.

Inside Animals

# Animal Parasites

This microscopic image of a louse shows the claws it uses to grip a human hair.

Parasites that live on the bodies of other animals usually have tiny claws, hooks, suckers, or teeth to grab on to their hosts. Lice are small, wingless insects that feed on blood. Head lice have claws that hook over human hairs, so they are very hard to dislodge. They lay eggs called nits, which cause itching. Lice can be passed on by close contact

### ? Did You Know?

Most parasites are smaller than their hosts. However, the tapeworms that live in human intestines can grow up to 33 feet (10 m) long. The tapeworm sticks to the wall of the intestines using suckers on its head.

# Pests and Parasites

between humans, or by sharing clothes, hairbrushes, or bedding.

## Ticks and mites

Ticks and mites are tiny relatives of spiders. They feed on blood or skin. Sheep ticks climb aboard passing animals, drill into their host with their barbed mouthparts, and feast on their blood. When the body of the tick is swollen with blood, it drops off. Deer ticks can cause a serious disease called Lyme disease.

Mites are even smaller than ticks. One type, called dust mites, are tiny parasites that live in dust and feed on dead skin cells. Some humans are allergic to dust mites and may suffer from breathing problems. Dust mites are so small that they are very difficult to see and remove.

## Fast Facts

- Lampreys are parasitic fish with suckerlike mouths. They latch onto other fish and feast on their flesh and blood.

- Some wasps lay their eggs inside caterpillars. When the wasps hatch, they eat the caterpillar from the inside out.

## Bloodsuckers

Fleas are tiny wingless insects that suck the blood of animals such as cats, dogs, and humans. Adult fleas live on the bodies of their hosts. They use their piercing mouthparts to penetrate the skin and suck up the host's blood.

The soft body of this sheep tick is swollen with blood. A sheep tick can expand by up to ten times its normal size when full of blood.

43

Inside Animals

# Bacteria and Viruses

Bacteria and viruses are tiny parasites that live in or on the bodies of almost all animals. Some are harmless, but others cause disease. Bacteria and viruses are so small that scientists need powerful microscopes to look at them.

## Bacteria

There are more bacteria in the world than any other group of living things. Some bacteria are slender, rod-shaped organisms, while others are tiny balls. Many bacteria are useful. For example, the bacteria that live inside a cow's stomach break down grass and help the cow digest its food. Others bring deadly diseases, such as tuberculosis. Most animals have a range of defences against these deadly bacteria. They include a natural barrier, such as the skin, and bacteria-fighting white blood cells that engulf the invaders. Disease occurs when the growth of the bacteria spirals out of control.

## Viruses

Viruses are so small that scientists need to use powerful microscopes to look at them. Viruses invade body cells and force them to produce more virus cells. When the body cell dies, the viruses burst out of the cell and spread to other cells.

These rod-shaped bacteria, called *Escherichia coli,* or *E. coli* are living in a cow's stomach.

44

Pests and Parasites

# Conclusion

Animals come in many different shapes and sizes, live in different parts of the world, and reproduce in different ways. But whatever their differences, all animals share one feature—they are made up of tiny cells.

The chemical reactions that take place inside cells drive every living process inside an animal's body. Cells need oxygen and fuel in the form of food to keep an animal alive.

Some cells work together as tissues. Muscle tissues contract and relax to help different animals move in an amazing variety of ways. Cells and tissues group up to form structures called organs, such as eyes, that help animals make sense of their surroundings.

Scientists can now study the invisible world inside animals. They are using microscopes to look at cells. These powerful microscopes reveal even the smallest structures inside animals, and help us to understand the way they work.

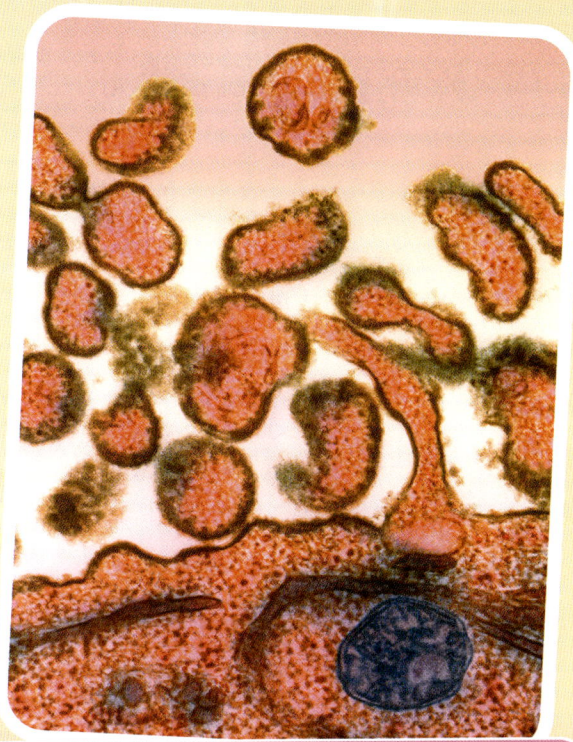

This picture shows measles viruses bursting out through the membrane of an infected cell.

## Viruses and disease

Viruses cause many diseases, from the common cold to chickenpox. Some viruses are destroyed by body defenses such as white blood cells. Medicines called vaccines can also be used to prevent some viruses from causing diseases. One virus, called human immunodeficiency virus (HIV), causes a disease called AIDS, which destroys the body's ability to fight off illness.

# Glossary

**alveoli** These tiny air sacs are the sites of gaseous exchange in the lungs—oxygen passes into the blood, while carbon dioxide passes back out into the lungs.

**cells** These microscopic structures make up the bodies of animals and other living things.

**clones** A clone is any living thing produced without sexual reproduction.

**cytoplasm** This jellylike material surrounds the nucleus of a cell.

**digestion** The process of digestion is when animals break down and absorb nutrients from food.

**fertilization** This process of fertilization occurs when a sperm joins with an egg.

**genes** Chemical instructions called genes help to build the bodies of living things.

**hermaphrodites** Animals that are both male and female are called hermaphrodites.

**host** A host is an animal that has a parasite living on or in its body.

**membrane** This thin wall surrounds a body part such as a cell.

**metamorphosis** This dramatic body change occurs when some animals develop into adults.

**nerves** Bundles of fibers called nerves carry electrical signals around the body.

**organelle** An organelle is part of a cell that does a particular job.

**organisms** An organism is any living thing, such as an animal.

**organs** Groups of cells and tissues are called organs. They do particular jobs in the body.

**parasites** Animals that live on or in other animals and steal their nutrients are called parasites.

**parthenogenesis** This form of reproduction occurs when an egg develops into an animal without being fertilized.

**respiration** This process occurs when animals take in oxygen and get rid of waste carbon dioxide.

**species** A species is a type of animal that can only breed with an animal of the same kind.

**sperm** The sperm is the male sex cell.

**tissues** Collections of cells, called tissues, all do the same job.

# Find Out More

## Books

*Amazing Animals Q & A.* New York: DK Publishing, 2007.

Gray, Leon, and John Woodward. *Ocean Life.* London, England: Brown Bear Books, 2007.

Hickman, Pamela. *Animal Senses: How Animals See, Hear, Taste, Smell and Feel.* Toronto, Ontario: Kids Can Press, Ltd., 2008.

Kallman, Bobbie, and Rebecca Sjonger. *Metamorphosis: Changing Bodies.* New York: Crabtree Publishing Company, 2008.

Siganowicz, Igor. *Animals Up Close.* New York: DK Publishing, 2009.

Tilden, Thomasine. *Belly-Busting Worm Invasions!: Parasites That Love Your Insides!* Boston, Massachusetts: New York: Franklin Watts, 2008.

## Websites

http://www.bbc.co.uk/nature/animals/
The BBC website is for anyone interested in animals and the natural world around them. The site includes special features such as fact files, quizzes, and screensavers.

http://www.mnh.si.edu/explore.html
Take a tour of the Smithsonian National Museum of Natural History website. Click on the Diversity of Life link to find out about a range of animal groups, past and present.

http://www.under-microscope.com/lifeforms/animal_cells/
Examine a range of different cells under the microscope—from human blood cells to the ovaries of a cat—at this website.

# Index

Page numbers in **boldface** are illustrations.

antenna, of a moth, 30
ants, **11, 21**
aphids, 35, **37**

bacteria, 10, 40, **44**
birds, 10, 13, 16, 20, 24, 36, 37
   feathers, 24, **25**
blood, 8, 12, 13, 17, 40, 41, 42, 43, 44, 45
   cells, 8, **13, 41,** 44, 45
bones, 10, 11, 18, 20
   skeletons, 10, 11
brain, 18, 26, 29, 31
breathing, 12, 16–17
butterflies, **25,** 38, **39**

carbon dioxide, 17
caterpillars, 16, 38, 43
cells, 6–11, 12, **13,** 15, 16, 18, 26, 28–29, 31, 32, **33,** 35, 36, 37, 38, 40, **41,** 43, 44, 45
   division, 8, 35, 36
   membrane, 6, 9, 45
   nuclei, 8, 9, 32, 45
   organelles, 8–9, 45
circulatory system, 12, 13
clones, 34, 37

digestion, 10, 12, 14–15
diseases, 10, 40, 44, 45
dogs, **10,** 30, 31, 40
dolphins, 23, **29**
dragonflies, 25, **28**

ears, 29
echolocation, **29**
eggs, 32, **33,** 35, **36,** 37, **38,** 39, 42

eyes, 15, 26, 27, **28,** 29, 32, 45

fish, 10, 11, 16, 17, **19,** 22, 23, 31, 36, 43
   lateral line, 31
   muscles, **19**
fleas, 20, 40, 43
flies, **15, 20, 21,** 31
food, 4, 6, 10, 12–15, 16, 18, 24, 26, 29, 31, 40, 45
frogs, 10, 17, 20, 35, 36, 37, **38, 39**
   tadpoles, **38,** 39

genes, 32
gills, 16, **17**

heart, 10, 12
hummingbirds, **24**
hydras, 26, 32, **34,** 35

insects, 11, 16, 20, 21, 23, 24, 25, 28, 30, 31, 35, 38, 42, 43

Jacobson's organs, **31**
jellyfish, 22, **23,** 26, 32

lice, 40, **42**
lizards, 20, 35
lungs, 16, 17
   alveoli, 17

mammals, 8, 9, 10, 16, 17, 20, 37, 38
metamorphosis, 38–39
mice, **27,** 30
microscopes, 4, 8, 15, 16, 41, 44, 45

mites, 40, 43
muscles, 10, 18, **19,** 22, 23, 25, 45

nerves, 18, 26

organs, 10, 26, 31
oxygen, 12, 13, 16–17, 45

parasites, 40–45
plants, 4, 6, 10, 12, 14, 15
predators, 15, 18, 26, 29, 35
protists, 10, **41**

radula, of a snail, **14**
reproduction, 32–39
rotifers, 6, **7**

senses, 4, 26–31
sharks, 11, 17, 22, 30
   scaly skin, **22**
snakes, 10, 18, 21, 27, **30, 31**
sperm, 32, **33,** 35, 36, 37
spiracles, **16**
starfish, 22, 26, **35**

ticks, 40, **43**
tissues, 10, 16, 45

vaccines, 45
viruses, 40, 44, **45**

water fleas, **4–5**
whales, 6, 14, 17, 22, 23
wings, 20, 24, 25
worms, 11, 18, 21, 31, 35, 40, 42

X rays, **10**

48